8

Survival

Secrets

OTHER BOOKS BY STEVEN HILFERTY

Small Business Coaching

8 Simple Secrets for Small Business Owners

8 Survival Secrets

for Small Business Owners

By Steven Hilferty

Business Coach Press
Alamo, California

8 SURVIVAL SECRETS
FOR SMALL BUSINESS OWNERS

Copyright © 2009 by Steven Hilferty

ISBN: 978-0-9789627-1-5

Library of Congress Control Number: 2009928534

Send permission requests to:
Permissions
Business Coach Press
48 Mathews Place
Alamo, CA 94507
Or email to: info@8survivalsecrets.com

Manufactured in the United States of America

9 8 7 6 5 4 3 2 1

TABLE OF CONTENTS

Introduction

Walt couldn't put it off any longer, he had to call his Virtual Executive Assistant and break the news to her.

After Sherry answered, he got right to the point, saying: "I need to cut back on the work you are doing for me. I know we agreed to a minimum of 10 hours per week, but I don't have any more work for you now. I hope you understand."

"Of course I do, Walt," Sherry replied. "I have other small business clients who have also cut back spending. In fact, I had to let one of my own part-time contractors go. Fortunately, he was in his last year at the university and needed extra time to study."

"Thanks for understanding," Walt said, relieved she had taken it so well.

"But Walt," Sherry went on, "I thought your business was doing very well. Other small businesses have been hit hard during this industry downturn. Your business, on the other hand, has customers from different industries. So, I assumed you had a *recession-proof* business."

After a pause, Walt explained, "Many people still need what I offer, Sherry, but everyone seems to be cutting back. One customer said she will not be reordering. Two more said they are waiting much longer between orders, and one is not even returning my calls."

When Sherry didn't say anything, he continued: "To make matters worse, I stupidly assumed I could keep selling in spite of changes to the economy, so I made some major expenditures over the last few months. Prices were so good that I just couldn't pass them up. If I only knew then what I know now."

"Don't be too hard on yourself," Sherry tried to console him. "Lots of very smart people were also fooled."

"It really doesn't matter, Sherry. My business, my life, seems ready to come crashing down if I don't get myself out of the hole I've dug. I have no idea what to do. I may have to declare bankruptcy if things don't turn around soon," Walt lamented.

"Who are you talking to about this type of decision?" Sherry asked, very concerned about how Walt sounded. "Do you have a business coach? How about a group of entrepreneurs you meet with? If not, who do you discuss your business decisions with?"

"My business has been going great since I started three years ago, so I haven't needed a business coach. I've been so busy that I've been pretty isolated from other business owners except when I see them at occasional networking events. It seems that my family and my customers are the only ones I've been talking to about much of anything. To be honest, it's been pretty lonely, but doable, until now..."

"Walt, I've got another good client, Helen, who lives near you. She is a very successful entrepreneur who is doing even better these days, in spite of these trying economic times. I'm going to call her today and see if she can meet with you."

"I'm not sure what it will do," Walt replied to the offer, "but I'm certainly willing to talk if you think that could help."

Helen was in her home office when Sherry called.

"Sherry, I'm so glad you called. I am going to send you another proposal that I need you to clean up. You know, do your magic that makes me look good. And I'll need it in two days..."

"Sure, Helen. I'm putting the finishing touches on that other project. But the main reason I called is to ask a favor: Another client of mine is going through some difficult times and needs someone to talk to. Of course I thought of you."

Helen looked around her office and sighed. Three piles of paper were propped on the edge of her desk. The cat was lying on potentially important papers in her inbox. And she knew the morning's mail would bring more paperwork that would need attention.

FOR SMALL BUSINESS OWNERS   5

"What I really need, Sherry, is to have someone straighten out my office. How would you like to come by while I'm in Omaha this week?"

With a laugh, Sherry replied, "I'd be glad to drive the three hours to get to you, as long as you find a way to get here, from Omaha, to pick up my kids from school and get them to their afternoon activities."

"I guess I'm doomed then," Helen concluded. "Okay. Tell me about this client of yours."

"His name is Walt. I've been doing Virtual Executive Assistant work for him for about a year, and he seems like a great guy. I've never met him because he lives in your city, but he is always accommodating to my schedule, clear about what he wants, and always pays on time. In other words, a great client for me."

"Then what's the problem?"

"He was doing great, but this economic upheaval, especially in your area, really surprised him. When I talked to him a little while ago, he was panicked about clients pulling back their contracts. He sounded so different that I'm concerned about him. When I asked him, he did not seem to have anyone to talk with. You can relate to what he's going through!"

Helen looked around the office and thought about her overly full schedule. Sighing one more time, she said, "You'll owe me for this, Sherry."

"What if I get that proposal done this afternoon?"

"I was thinking more about you coming here and cleaning my office," Helen replied, knowing she would only hear Sherry's laughter as an answer.

Helen had started her own business thirteen years ago, having worked as an employee for much too long, as she told it. Her timing was perfect, the products and services she provided were just becoming popular, and necessary for many businesses. She quickly built a company that was noticed by the movers and shakers in the city. In less than three years, she was nominated for "Entrepreneur of the Year" by the local business journal.

Unfortunately, she didn't see turbulent times approaching. A year after her nomination, Helen almost went bankrupt.

That was a dark time. She could not find any way out of the predicament she found herself in. She felt like a failure. If not for the support of friends and family, it could have been catastrophic.

During this era (it certainly felt like many years), Helen was introduced to a successful business owner who eventually became her mentor. This entrepreneur taught her many survival secrets, such as anticipating shifts in the economy, adjusting financial expectations and how to work *ON* the business instead of just *IN* the business. The only thing he asked in return was for her to pass this business knowledge on to others who needed it.

Starting Out

Walt had never been to the cafe that Helen suggested, although he had been to this part of town many times.

Traffic had been moving briskly, so he arrived fifteen minutes early to the light and airy setting. The atmosphere inside Yellow Wood was informal, which probably accounted for the variety of patrons he observed sitting, chatting and working at the well-spaced tables. Some men and women looked as if they were taking a break from high-powered corporate meetings, while others looked like students. Judging from the baby strollers, some parents were obviously meeting other parents. Walt noted the ones who probably worked out of their homes, judging from their casual attire while intensely working on laptops and shuffling through papers.

All in all, he decided it made a very comfortable meeting place. The staff was attentive, but not bothered by those who stayed for hours, as evidenced by the empty coffee cups strewn among papers as individuals typed away.

Walt ordered a large coffee and waited for Helen to arrive, as patiently as someone in his predicament could be.

He was lost in thought when a tap on his shoulder startled him. A confident woman smiled down at him. "Walt?" she asked.

Walt jumped to his feet. "Helen?" They shook hands and sat down. "What can I get you?" motioning for the waitress who was already on the way over.

Helen ordered tea and they chatted, mostly about Sherry and how much she helped each of them.

Once her tea had cooled enough to drink, Helen took a sip and then asked, "What can I do for you, Walt?"

"Sherry asked me to meet with you, I guess so I could learn a thing or two from you."

"Sherry is not particularly impressed with a lot of her clients, but you must have made the grade, Walt. She seemed worried about you and hoped that somehow I could help, but wasn't too clear about what that would be."

"Wow. I didn't know Sherry was 'impressed' with me. I just know she wanted me to listen to your advice, assuming it's not too late for my business. I would appreciate anything you have to offer."

Helen nodded and explained, "My business is very different from yours. However, I have been doing it for over ten years and managed to survive, while a lot of companies have come and gone."

Her background and confidence spoke volumes about the wisdom she had gained from both her mentor and from running her own enterprise. Walt decided it would be a smart move to listen to her. "I probably could learn a lot from you. Unfortunately, I don't have money at this point to pay you."

"No money required. I'm not a Business Coach as such, although I do believe in the profession. Business Coaches help a lot of companies stay out of trouble."

He showed some surprise, but Helen continued, "I learned the 8 Business Survival Secrets from a mentor who wouldn't take money, but insisted that I pass them on to deserving people. If you are willing to share your business issues with me, I'm willing to offer some advice. Of course, if I don't think you are putting in the necessary effort, I'll bow out."

Walt assured her, "I am very serious right now. If your 8 Business Survival Secrets will help me, I will invest whatever time it takes."

"Then let's get started. Tell me about your situation."

Walt explained that his business had done well for several years. He loved running his small company, loved being his own boss, and knew in his heart that he was still destined to bring his company to prosperity. But his early success made him overconfident, and he made some large purchases on credit.

When the economy started to shift, his positive cash flow dried up, and he had to start dipping into his savings. He had fallen victim to a variety of issues, including financial commitments, changing customer expectations and reduced budgets for his products, without much hope for near-term improvements.

"For a while, I just ignored the problem, hoping it would go away," Walt explained. "But when I had trouble meeting my bills, I realized I had to do something. Last Wednesday afternoon, I took all my bills and financial information, laid them out on my kitchen table, and started going through them. Within an hour, I realized things were worse than I thought. Just about the time I heard the bell in the hall strike four o'clock, it felt like the end of the world was arriving. I had shortness of breath, pounding pulse, and a bunch of adrenaline made me want to flee, but I had no place to go."

"You certainly have that moment clearly inscribed in your memory," Helen noted.

"Since then I haven't been able to sleep well, and don't know what to do," Walt admitted. "I know I should do something, but my brain doesn't seem to be able to make decisions right now, except for the decision to panic. I consider myself pretty cool and calm under pressure, but I don't know how to handle this."

He was close to tears as he finished, which embarrassed him, but he had rarely spoken honestly about the condition of his company.

Helen, however, gave him very little time to recover. She asked pointed questions to clarify the issues and she concluded, "Your business finances are so out of whack, they are affecting your whole life. No wonder you feel like you have no control." She explained, "You were making decisions based on what you thought was correct, but now realize you were relying on erroneous information. It seems to me that the first step is to take back some control."

"How can I do that?" Walt asked.

"By making decisions that will protect your future," she replied.

Survival Secret 1:
Minimize Expenditures

"Get back to that pile of papers on your kitchen table and make a list of all the places where you have been spending money," Helen directed. "Look at both your business and personal expenses. Making a concise list of your monthly expenditures is an important start to taking back control."

"I don't think that is going to help," Walt said, sounding defeated.

"It's the first step," Helen explained. "You are going to have to cut your expenses drastically, if things are as bad as you say. So you might as well see what those expenses are. Look at your records very carefully and identify every expense you can."

"But I'm too far over my head," Walt tried.

Helen quickly came back with, "How much over your head are you? What are your average monthly expenses on business supplies?"

"They vary a lot, month to month, so I'm not sure," Walt admitted.

"Then, how much do you spend on lattes and other minor expenses that aren't an absolute requirement of your business during the month?"

Walt had to acknowledge that he wasn't keeping close tabs on those expenses.

"And how much can your family cut back before they are seriously impacted?" Helen went on.

"I'm not really sure how much we spend on things."

"My point exactly," Helen gestured with her hands. "As a small business owner, you are responsible for making the important decisions that can keep the company alive, or kill it. You don't let other people make business decisions for you, do you?"

"No. I make my own decisions."

"Then take control of your expenses, too," Helen commanded. "And keep your family in the loop, too."

Walt swallowed hard at that, then said, "I guess you are right. I've been afraid to tell my family how bad things are right now. But keeping it to myself is eating me up inside."

"I am not surprised. As you discuss it with them, be prepared for some shocked reactions on your family's part. After all, while you have had weeks to digest it, they may be taken completely unaware. It will take away some control that they thought they had. But after a little bit, they will be ready to help make the situation better, too," Helen said confidently.

"You're right," Walt said, a bit morosely. "But what if I can't find enough expenses to cut? What then? I suppose I will have to declare bankruptcy..."

"Aren't you being a bit overdramatic?" Helen interjected. "After all, last Wednesday was the first time you even realized you were in trouble. At this point you don't even know how heavy a burden you have to carry. And you may have a lot of minor expenses you can cut, ones you didn't even notice before. Having a latte or two during the day seems pretty minor, but what would happen if you brewed some coffee at home, put it in a thermos, and used that instead. Would that be a huge tradeoff to save ten or twenty dollars every week?"

"No, it wouldn't be too bad. I could certainly survive," Walt agreed. "But it reminds me of the way my parents and grandparents scrimped on so many things. They worked but had to go without the extras. They had to cut coupons and shop the sales and do anything else to bring us up. I want my children to have it easier, and not suffer."

"That sounds pretty noble," Helen agreed. "But you still seem to have come out all right, in spite of your parents bringing you up without too many luxuries. You have been very successful in your career. You even started a business that did great for three years."

"I don't feel very successful right now," Walt countered. "And it's all because the bottom unexpectedly dropped out of the entire industry."

Helen pointed out, "This downturn we are going through now is very, very normal."

"Normal! I've never seen anything this bad before," Walt snorted.

"In that case, you must have been on a salary in past downturns that affected your industry," Helen guessed. "And you didn't lose your job because of the economy."

"I did have a pretty secure job in the last couple of market dips. And I wish I was still there now," Walt said sadly.

"To those of us who had a business, what you call a *market dip* seemed like an impassable abyss. Each dip was very dangerous for us. We prayed that our business could make it through to the next economy upturn. And we know plenty of businesses that could not hold on any more - they just plummeted into the abyss..."

"I ... I guess I never paid attention," he answered, feeling a bit guilty.

"Those of us who survived saw a pattern. A few years of good times were almost always followed by a wild downhill ride. We know they are coming, but we never know when. We just hope we have taken enough precautions to keep from getting pushed over the edge."

Walt looked surprised. "So you knew this was coming?"

"Sure, it only took me one time of getting smacked to understand the reality of economic ups and downs. Before then, I thought the best way to grow a business was to borrow money and buy things on credit while times were good. Oh, yeah, that's what the lenders want you to think," Helen said, almost angrily.

Then she continued softly, the sudden change got Walt's full attention: "Now I try to follow what Thomas Jefferson said two hundred years ago, *Never spend your money before you have earned it.*"

"Where was he when I was buying stuff?" Walt wondered out loud. "Then I wouldn't have gotten myself into this much trouble."

"Once you are out of trouble, I hope you remember and heed his saying," Helen went on.

"If I *can* get myself out of trouble," Walt corrected.

"You'll probably get past the issues you are in now, but it will be painful. I don't know of any easy way for people to get out of debt while, at the same time, learning not to do it again," Helen warned.

"I can take a little pain, but I'm not sure even where to go from here. If my cash flow is as out of whack as I think, what can I do?"

Helen looked serious as she explained, "Cutting costs is only the first step. You need to find some free cash, too. For example, "Do you have customers who are behind on payments?"

"I have a few that are," Walt shrugged.

"Then call them up. Let them know they are behind. Just calling is an easy way to get your invoice to the top of the pile to be paid. How about your creditors? Are you getting a good interest rate or are you paying a high rate?" was Helen's next question.

"Well, they are not the best, but I didn't worry too much about them."

"Call them up, too," Helen suggested. "See if you can negotiate lower interest rates. They may be having trouble getting people with good credit to borrow. Don't get behind on payments if you can possibly help it. Lenders want to immediately raise your payments as high as they can when you get behind because it is a signal of higher risk. When calling, you may NOT want to tell them you are experiencing financial difficulties, because that may give them the impression you are now an increased risk. As long as you act like you DON'T need the credit, they will frequently be willing to negotiate lower rates to keep you as a customer."

"How about the equipment I bought on credit. Would those rates be negotiable?" Walt asked.

"Of course they would. You have the equipment, the vendors only have an IOU. Give them a call and see what they are willing to negotiate, even an extended payment plan," Helen suggested.

"Okay, I'll give it a shot," Walt said hopefully. "Any more thoughts?"

"I've got a little cheat sheet that I use when things start to get tight, financially." She opened up a spiral-bound notebook from her bag and took out a folded sheet of paper. Checking to make sure it was the correct one, she handed it to him.

Before Walt got a chance to look through it, she told him, "Unfortunately, I have to run to a meeting on the other side of town. I put you on my schedule to meet here again next week. Will that work for you?"

"Sure. Thanks! That would be great. "

"See you then," and she walked off.

Suddenly Walt realized he had better check his calendar, since he had committed Helen's time. He had one appointment that conflicted with next week's meeting, but the meeting with Helen was much more important. So he rescheduled the conflict to keep his meeting time with her and provide, hopefully, some solution to his predicament.

Then he looked at the sheet of paper she had given him and read:

8 Tips to Minimize Expenditures

1. Record all expenses, personal and financial.

2. Ruthlessly eliminate everything not absolutely necessary.

3. List all recurring bills and debts to understand how much money you will need, and when.

4. Keep a journal of all ordinary expenses for several weeks, preferably a month, to show your "hidden expenses."

5. Contact all customers who owe you money and remind them that payments are due.

6. Call lenders to get best rates available.

7. Shop around and renegotiate with service providers to get the best rates possible.

8. Keep your loved ones involved.

Walt was seated in Yellow Wood before Helen arrived, with his financial papers at the ready.

Once she sat down and ordered, Walt explained, "My situation is not as bad as I feared. I can cut a fair amount of expenses from my business, although I'll still have to do more to survive until this economy strengthens, I'm afraid. So on Saturday, I told my family that business was way down and we needed to cut our family budget. Our standard of living was going to have to change. I expected tears or panic, but nobody was particularly surprised, which surprised me. Since we could still stay in the house and continue with most of the things that we had before, they accepted it and moved on - in less than half an hour. After all my worrying, it was pretty anti-climactic," Walt admitted.

Helen asked, "How do you feel this week, compared to last week?"

"Last week, I was in a panic. This week I'm ready to roll up my sleeves and get to work."

"Then let's do it!" Helen agreed.

Survival Secret 2:
Hang Onto Customers

Helen began, "Now that you have tackled your costs, let's look at your revenue. What are you doing to protect your revenue?"

"Well, I am doing everything I can to stay in business. But what do you mean by *protect* my revenue?" Walt asked, a bit confused.

Helen explained, "By *protect*, I mean hanging onto as many of your current customers as you possibly can. What are you doing to encourage them to start buying from you again?"

"The problem is that most of my clients are not calling," Walt explained. "I need to get out there more and get new customers. I'm not sure what the most cost-effective way to do that would be."

"Do you know that it costs about five times as much to get a new customer as it does to keep an existing one?" Helen paused to let that sink in. "Ignoring existing clients means higher *costs* to get new clients for probably less *revenue*. That equates to a smaller *profit*. Can you afford that now?"

"Of course not," Walt replied. Then under his breath, "That's why I need advice from you!" Afraid he had said it too loud, he apologized, "I'm sorry, Helen, you just threw me a curve here, and I'm a little jumpy."

Helen just looked at him, so Walt continued, "Okay, I'm open to what you have to say."

Helen tried again. "Getting new customers takes a lot of time or money, or both. You are in a pretty severe cash flow problem, from what you are saying, so the sooner and cheaper you get some revenue in, the sooner you can get past this problem. Your customers already know you, have done business with you, and may be open to doing more business if you offer them the right value. Tell me what you know about them," she directed.

"I know that they are not buying from me. In fact, most of them are not buying from any vendor. They've been hit hard by this change in the economy. That's why I need to find new customers, and I need to get them cheaply."

Helen reminded him, "Keep in mind that the same economic conditions that are affecting your existing customers are also affecting the new customers you are trying to reach. That makes it even more difficult, and more expensive, to convince new people to buy from you."

"I forgot about that," Walt admitted.

"Then let's focus on those who have already purchased from you," the experienced entrepreneur said as she steered the conversation back. "How do you keep in touch with them?"

"I really haven't," Walt replied sheepishly. "Until recently, I've been so busy that I haven't had time to touch base with them. I'm waiting for them to call me."

The look he got said it all. "I know my business would have been better if I kept in contact, but what can I do now?"

"Woo them," was Helen's reply.

"Woo them?" Walt was taken aback. "Woo them? Like asking them out on a date?"

"More like treating them very, very special. Like they are the most important customers in the world because, to you, they probably are. These are the ones who can keep your business going until the economy improves. These are the ones who can send referrals your way," Helen explained. "But they can only help you if they remember you. So, you need to contact them."

"But what should I say when I haven't talked to them in months?"

Helen answered the question with a question, "What do you have for a customer relationship management system?"

"A what?"

"You know, some sort of system you use to keep track of the last time you contacted a client, their birthdays, what products they bought?"

"I've got it in my head..." Walt replied hopefully.

"You need a system. Sales professionals call it a Customer Relationship Management system, or CRM for short. Many of the computer calendars and address books have adequate features built in. Up until a few years ago, I still used a paper and pen for my CRM. Once my list got too big, I had to go electronic. Whatever you choose, find *something* to help you maintain a relationship with your customers."

"I guess the address book on my computer will do for now. But the customers I haven't talked to in a long time...?"

"I assume you have friends and family members that you don't keep up with regularly. How do you start conversations with them after a long time?"

"I feel guilty, of course, but they feel guilty, too. In a minute or two we get past the awkwardness. But what about business associates?" Walt wondered.

"If you treat customers like friends, you'll be okay," Helen assured him. "Ask them how they are doing. People love to talk about themselves, as long as the listener is genuinely interested. In other words, this is not a sales call. This is a call to rekindle a relationship with a VIP. If you make it about yourself, they probably don't have time for it. If you make it about them, they will find a way to make time. If not now, then soon."

"Are you sure they will want to hear from me?"

Helen explained, "As long as you have not alienated them somehow, most will be delighted to hear from you. The hard part is just picking up the phone."

"True. But even if I do, how will asking about their lives get me more business?"

"They know you are not just calling to hear about their lives, they know you need business, too."

"Sometimes people act like I am a bill collector or something. What do I do then?" he inquired.

"People are very busy, and when they haven't heard from you in a long time, may be suspicious that you are only interested in their check book. So put them at ease," Helen explained.

"But I don't want to be a bother by calling them," was Walt's next objection.

"Then make sure you are not bothering them. Ask them if now is a convenient time to talk. If not, find a more convenient time. If they agree to a time, chances are they will be willing to talk to you then."

"But even then, I'm afraid I will be bothering them. I know I hate to talk to sales reps, unless I really need something," he countered.

"Many sales professionals discuss themselves and their products, and the customers don't even enter into their equation, except to give them money. If you show a real interest in your customers, they will be quite open. I tend to follow the FORD method."

"The FORD method?" Walt was confused.

"That's right, FORD is an acronym. F is for Family, O is for Occupation, R is for Recreation, and D is for Dreams. You can ask people about their family, and if that doesn't seem appropriate you can ask how their company, their occupation, is doing these days."

Walt picked up on that, "Or I can ask about their weekend or vacations. But I'm not sure what to do with Dreams."

Helen thought a moment before answering. "After you've established some sort of relationship, you can develop a closer rapport by asking questions like, *Where do you see yourself in a few years?* or *If you had all the money and time you wanted, what would you do?*"

"Even so, I have trouble doing that small talk stuff," Walt admitted. "I still want to get straight to the point."

Helen nodded. "You can, of course, take the dangerous path and start talking about your products."

"Dangerous? Why is that dangerous?" Walt's queried.

"It's dangerous because they find out you are only looking to make a sale. In that case, they may immediately write you off. For instance, if you say you are really calling to let them know about a special you are running, they can easily say they don't need it and end the conversation. You will have squandered a very important opportunity to have them think of you as more than a sales person or a vendor."

"I see your point," Walt acknowledged. "I'm just not used to being personal with business associates."

"Maybe, but taking a genuine interest in clients is very important for business owners," Helen reiterated. "You depend on these people, and need them to like you. Talk about things that are important to them. You may not want to be best friends with all your customers, but you've got to be some sort of friend to most of them. Then they want to do business with you. They will even tell you ahead of time what opportunities will be coming."

"I guess you are right," Walt agreed. "But when do I discuss my products?"

"Not on the first sales call. If you don't want to talk about non-work items, you could ask if any issues have come up with your product since the last time you talked. Then see what you can do to resolve those issues. Even spending some time on the telephone doing some troubleshooting will get your foot in the door for repeat business and, possibly, some referrals." Helen coached.

"Do I need to make a series of calls?" Walt asked, knowing the answer.

"That's right. The secret is to get customers to take your calls, even when they aren't going to buy," Helen confirmed. "The more you are on their mind, the more likely they will think of you when situations come up in which your services would be helpful."

"How can I get them to give me more referrals, Helen?"

"How about a Referral Program? You could offer the person giving you the referral some recognition, such as cash, discounts, points, or whatever."

"But won't people be insulted if I offer them money in return for referring me to their friends and colleagues?"

"Again, you need to be subtle. A lot of acquaintances are willing to give your name out, if the subject comes up. What you need is to get them to give *you* names of people who probably need your product, and to allow you to use their name. Some are more willing if they get something in return. Others, however, do not want a reward for themselves. They would prefer their referral get a discount. Keep in mind that different rewards motivate different people."

"Okay, I'll be subtle. What else, Helen?"

"Write up a script for your calls. I have to admit that I don't always think that fast on my feet. If I have a script for the phone call, then I am not fazed if voice mail comes on, or if someone else answers the phone, or if they sound grouchy when they answer."

"Does it get any easier?"

Helen smiled. "Yes, it gets easier the more I do it. But I still like to keep my scripts handy. When something gets me off track, I refer to my script to get me back. In your case, you'll need a series of scripts because you'll use one for the first call, another for the second, third and so forth."

"But don't scripts sound mechanical and forced," Walt asked.

"Not if you practice them. Write one, and then practice it. If it doesn't sound like the natural you, change it until it does. Then practice, practice, practice. The more you practice, the more natural it sounds. It may be counterintuitive, but the more you practice, the more sincere and spontaneous you will sound."

"I should have taken theater in high school," Walt muttered. "Okay, I've got it: Practice until I sound sincere. What else can I do, Helen?"

"After you've reestablished a relationship with your customers, you can go over the items on your checklist."

That puzzled Walt. "Checklist? What checklist?"

"The one you are going to make, of course," Helen explained. "Make a checklist so you can continue to enhance your relationship, not only with the clients you are talking to at the time, but the rest of your clients, and new prospective clients. Here's one I've used in the past when touching base with customers," Helen said as she handed him a folded sheet of paper. "I've got to run. This block of time works well for me, Walt, if you want to meet here next week."

"I've already got it on my calendar, Helen. I was hoping it would work for you."

As she walked away, Walt unfolded the sheet and read:

8 Ways to Hang Onto Customers

1. Create a "customer relationship management" system to keep in regular contact with customers.

2. Develop a script, then pick up the phone and call.

3. Get personal - make it about them. You can use the FORD method: Family, Occupation, Recreation, Dreams.

4. Remember that things may have changed, so find out what their needs are today. Then you can show how your product will help meet some of those needs.

5. Identify new ways to help your clients. Ask questions like: "What would you like us to do differently?"

6. Find out how your product has been working for them.

7. Offer a Referral Reward Program.

8. Set up a repeat buyer program, such as a reduced price for two or more things purchased at the same time, or Reward Cards for points and discounts.

The following week, Helen was talking to a woman when Walt arrived.

When Helen noticed him, she waved him over. "Walt, I'd like you to meet Lauren, the owner of Yellow Wood."

Walt shook her hand and said, "At least you seem to be doing great in this economy."

Lauren looked at the people sitting at the tables, working on laptops or chatting. Then she murmured, "Looks can be deceiving. We have had a significant drop in revenue over the last few months. Even though the number of orders had been fairly steady, the amount of each order is only a fraction of what it was before. People who used to order dessert are now going without. Others are ordering drip coffee instead of lattes."

Walt was taken aback. "Wow. I guess I was just looking at the obvious signs. Will you survive?"

Lauren gave him a wry smile, "We'll get by for now. We're not paying much rent, and we've found other ways to cut costs. But there will be no Hawaiian vacation for a while."

Then she turned to his mentor and said, "Thanks again, Helen. I know I can always get solid advice from you." Then, with a wave to Walt, she was off.

After Walt ordered some coffee and got settled, Helen asked, "How did your week go?"

"The good news is that I made a few phone calls, and nobody hung up on me."

Helen's face lit up while he talked. "You talked to some clients? Many owners dread doing that, so they use any excuse to keep from making the call."

Walt admitted, "That was me, too. But you convinced me of the importance of keeping existing customers. The bad news is that nobody seems to be ready to buy right now. I got the same story again and again: They are afraid to make ANY purchases that are not absolutely necessary until they are sure the economy is on the mend."

Walt's voice took on a worried tone as he relayed this information. "Several of them told me they don't have any idea when they will be ready to buy. This quarter? Next quarter? Next year? At this point, I'm not sure I even have a viable business," he conceded.

Helen nodded, "Then let's start talking about the third Survival Secret."

Survival Secret 3:
Revise Your Business Model

"If you can't sell products to your existing clients," Helen began, "you need to take a close look at your business model. Is it still valid?"

"My business model? What do you mean by *model*?" Walt asked.

"Your business model is the method of doing business, how you add value to customers and create revenue," Helen explained. "It's the foundation on which you run your company."

"Do you mean like a building foundation, what a house sits on?"

"Absolutely correct. If your house is on a solid foundation, it can last for many, many years. If the foundation is weak, some strong winds or flooding can quickly destroy an otherwise solid house."

Walt pondered that analogy. "So, if my house, my company, is built on a poor foundation, it could fall apart quickly under the right conditions."

Going on, he muttered, "I've built my company on a lousy foundation."

She paused the conversation by taking a sip of her tea. When she felt he was back on the same wavelength she went on, "You started with the idea that certain people would buy your product, you could deliver that product, and you would make money. Is that right?"

"I guess that was my thinking in a nutshell," Walt replied. "I spent more time on it than that, of course, and even developed a business plan, although I haven't really looked at it in three years. After I wrote it, I started delivering, and I've been too busy to update it."

"At least you have a business plan," Helen replied. "Many, perhaps even most, small businesses are started without a written plan at all. Since you have one, it will make this Survival Secret easier to implement. We can use your business plan as the start of the *business model* you are using now. Take out your plan, dust it off, and look it over."

"It probably has dust on it, all right," was his response.

"You should be looking at your business model at least every six months or so. That way, you will see flaws in your model or the underlying assumptions before you enter dangerous conditions."

After another pause, she continued, "It's a lot like riding a raft down a river with your family."

That metaphor took Walt by surprise. He mulled it over, then smiled at some memories. "I did go rafting with my family a couple of years ago. And I'm sure ready to do something fun again!"

Helen pointed out, "It would be fun, if nothing out of the ordinary happened. But what if things ahead aren't as calm as you assume. What if you missed some potential dangers when planning the trip?"

"I was very well prepared for that trip, thank you very much," Walt defended. "I checked the maps, read guidebooks, and talked to people who had done it before."

"I'm sure you did, Walt. But unexpected things still happen. What if a dam had been built since the guidebooks were published? Or perhaps, over the winter, a rockslide caused rapids to form where previously it had been calm. Maybe an overnight thunderstorm flooded a tributary, causing a major whirlpool where it joins the main river."

"Well, of course I can't plan for everything," Walt argued. "If I didn't take any chances, I'd never get out of the house."

"You were not very prepared for the potential dangers in the business environment."

"How could I have been? They caught me completely by surprise."

Helen explained, "Let's use the rafting example. Your family's life is in your hands. Do you just go drifting down the river, falling asleep with the gentle splashing of the waves?

Or, are you constantly looking ahead for danger?"

"A little of both I guess. If I don't see any danger ahead, I tend to relax."

Helen replied, "That's good. You can relax while the foreseeable future is calm. But every time you go around a bend of that river, you should be looking for conditions that are different than you expected. If you are not proactive, you won't see the tell tale signs of danger, ones that should be obvious a mile away."

"And if I am looking, I can take action early," Walt was catching on. "I can get to the side of the river before getting to those dangerous conditions. But what if I still have to continue down the river, to get to my destination?"

"You can do it one of two ways: Just keep going to stay on schedule, which could get you tossed around in the rapids, your equipment lost, your leg broken, or worse. Alternatively, keeping your eyes open for changing conditions, you can adjust your schedule and get prepared. Moving to the bank of the river, you can wait and observe. Maybe you can scout out the best route between the rocks. You could ask others what they know. You might even find a road nearby which goes around the rapids, so you can leisurely finish your journey. The important point is that you will be entering the dangerous areas prepared instead of being caught by surprise."

"And a periodic review of my business model can do that?"

"Absolutely! When you put your business plan together three years ago, you made a lot of assumptions. Now you've got working knowledge, so you can replace many of those assumptions with facts, based on your experience."

Walt allowed, "Yes, I can update it based on my experience over the last couple of years. But conditions have changed in ways I don't understand. How valid could my plan be now?"

Helen instructed, "Update it with what you know about doing business in this economy.

You will be using some facts, and then making more assumptions about what you think will be happening in the next couple of months."

"Ugh! I hate making too many assumptions. You know what they say when you *assume*," Walt joked.

"Yes, I do," Helen said, smiling. "But you need to make some assumptions to envision the future. Don't be overly optimistic, but make assumptions. Of course, you will want to validate those assumptions as soon as you can. At that point, you can update your model again and keep moving forward."

"But there are a number of successful business owners who never had a business plan. Could I be over-planning?"

She shrugged her shoulders, "You don't have to take my word for it. How about President Dwight Eisenhower? When head of Allied operations in Europe during World War II, he is famous for saying, '*In preparing for battle I have always found that plans are useless, but planning is indispensable.*' In other words, once in the thick of battle, many of the prior assumptions prove to be wrong. However, while planning the operation, participants are forced to consider different scenarios. The practice puts them in a position to make excellent decisions as the situation changes."

"Okay, okay, okay," Walt conceded with a smile. "I was planning to do it anyway. I just wanted to hear what else you had to say. So once I update my business plan, what else should I do to *validate* it?" was Walt's next question.

"*Validating your business model* is bringing together your knowledge, your products, your customers, their buying habits, and the niche of the economy you have chosen as your market. After putting them all together, ask yourself whether your products still make sense for your customers today."

"And if they don't?"

She responded, "We already know you have to change something. Let's take a look at the four options you have when things aren't going as planned. I'll draw you a little diagram."

Helen took a napkin from the table and drew:

		Products	
		Same	**New**
Customers	**Existing**	OPTION 1 Same products to existing customers	OPTION 2 New products to exisitng customers
	New	OPTION 3 Same products to new customers	OPTION 4 New Products to new customers

"Your first option is to keep selling the same products to your existing customers. That has the highest chance of success. In that case, you only need to tweak your business model. For instance, twenty years ago, if you were selling desks to large offices that had a lot of staff, you could make a pretty good living. Each person working in an office needed some sort of desk, from executive to stenographer. When people reduced spending on desks due to economic changes, you could still go to the same clients who worked with you before, and therefore trusted you, and you could offer discounts or other incentives to continue getting their business."

Walt interjected, "Like wooing your existing clients to keep them buying the same products, right?"

"Correct. A second option would be to go to the same customers and convince them to buy cubicles, a new product, to save space and money. They would certainly listen to you because they know and trust you."

"Selling new products to existing customers," nodded Walt.

"Your third option is to find new customers, such as businesses with smaller offices. As an expert with years in the desk industry, you could take a quick look at the layout and tell them exactly what they could use that would be efficient and cost effective."

"Selling the same products to new customers," Walt observed.

"The fourth, and riskiest, option would be to try to sell cubicles into small offices. While it is possible to convince them to change to cubicles, it would be harder justifying the cost efficiencies. Therefore it would be a tougher sell, especially since they don't know you."

"That's for sure. I'd probably be out of business pretty soon if I tried to sell those new products to new customers. Not much reward in that story," Walt concluded.

Helen held up her hand, "Unless you saw that the world was downsizing. If you saw small businesses moving rapidly to computers, you could provide a new product, such as computer desks with printer shelves. That could allow firms to downsize and save money on office rent. Then you could do very well, indeed."

"Okay, I see your point. Only if I see a great opportunity should I try to sell new products to new clients."

"That's right. And that is the purpose of reexamining your business model. Just keep in mind the objective of looking at your business model is NOT to make changes. The main reason is to take a fresh look at your business."

"And if I see a great opportunity?"

"You don't want to change just because something initially appears promising. New opportunities are usually much harder to take advantage of than they initially appear. What you want to do is take a slow, hard look at how you can make your business model better. Keep your eyes open, but your reactions slow."

"Walt, let's meet at the same time next week. I've got to run to my other appointment now, but here are 8 Steps I use to look at my business model on a regular basis," and Helen handed him a sheet of paper as she picked up her bag to leave.

8 Steps to Revise Your Business Model

1. Accurately assess your current business. What are you selling? Who is buying? Does it still make sense in today's conditions?

2. Determine what has been working. (This step is very important).

3. Look at what is not working, and see if minor changes fix these issues.

4. Forecast how many of your customers will continue to buy your products in the foreseeable future.

5. Identify other high-potential customers who may need your products.

6. Talk to your customers. Confirm your assumptions.

7. Keep your eyes open for new opportunities.

8. Make a decision of how your business should operate moving forward.

That evening, Walt took out the business plan he had written three years ago. Within a few minutes the memories of the hard work writing it became clear. As he read through it, he was surprised to see how different the reality of his business had been compared with what he expected at the time.

He had learned a great deal and had adapted to his clients' needs over the years. The *business model* he had been using for several years was very different from the *business plan* originally drafted.

But now, the business climate is so different from anything he had dealt with before, he was ill-prepared to forecast what changes would help his company survive.

Before long, he had to put the plan down. At that point it felt like he was in a small raft being tossed about by swift currents in a raging river without any oars for control. He was on the verge of being overturned into the cold, dark, muddy waters of reality.

The next day he ignored the plan on his desk, even "accidentally" dropping papers to hide it.

On the third day, realizing it needed to be updated before his next meeting with Helen, he retrieved it from under the bills and started the revisions.

The evening before his meeting with Helen, he realized the revised plan actually had a slim chance of success. It felt like he had found a small paddle to help him steer as the river of life rapidly carried him toward an unknown destination.

"Here is my new model, Helen," he began. "I have to admit that I'm not convinced it still fits for this economy, but at least I can see some pros and cons to the different options you mentioned last week."

Helen nodded, so he went on. "My problem is that my existing clients are still not ordering what I am selling. Is there something I am missing?"

Helen explained, "That is a major secret to surviving today's conditions."

Survival Secret 4: Offer New Products to Existing Customers

"What customers buy during times of uncertainty is very different from what they buy during good times," Helen explained. "When people feel confident, they buy all sorts of things for all sorts of reasons, some strong and some flimsy. But when they lose confidence and feel their standard of living is in danger, they immediately cut back discretionary spending and *hunker down* until their confidence returns.

"Hunker down?"

"That is a slang term for only doing things required for survival. People *hunker down* when major storms hit, riding it out until the weather clears. They also hunker down when economic storms hit and stop spending on anything unnecessary. Of course, they still need items such as food, water, clothing, housing and security."

"My products are not on that list," Walt pointed out. "So how can I sell if customers are hunkered down?"

"You probably have to expand your product line to things they still need, Walt."

"Expand my product line? You mean sell new things to existing customers?" Walt hoped to hear some more gems of wisdom.

"This survival secret is finding products that people still want or need to buy, even when they are not financially secure," Helen announced. "What can you offer your existing clients that they need to buy?"

"I'm not sure."

"The easiest way to find out is to ask your customers," Helen patiently explained.

"You mean I should just call them up and ask what they need?"

"Something like that. Of course, if you are too direct, people may feel you are pressuring them. I find it easier to have a pleasant conversation, no sales pressure, and keep my ears open," Helen explained.

"Is there another way to ask them?" Walt was grasping for anything that would keep these conversations to a minimum.

"If you ask more general, open-ended questions and listen carefully, they will tell you a lot about their needs."

"But that assumes that one customer's needs are valid for all my customers."

"You need to judge how valid it is. You have enough experience to trust your own instincts."

"My instincts haven't been working too well lately," Walt replied ruefully.

"Just because you haven't experienced some things doesn't mean you should discount the things you have experienced. Trust your gut. Here's an exercise for you: Sit at home, or in the park, or wherever works best for you, and think about your clients. What are their needs? What will they require? Write it down, in pencil if you'd like, then ask some of them. That way you get to test your assumptions. If you are right, they'll think you are a genius."

"Do you think so?"

Helen smiled and relaxed her posture. "I might have been lucky when I guessed in the past. But even when I was wrong, my clients were impressed that I'm trying to foresee their needs."

Walt relaxed along with her, leaning back in the booth and taking a break from the notes he had been scribbling. After a sip of coffee, he picked up the notes and read through them. "What do I do if they still don't buy? I guess I could negotiate new prices for them..."

Helen cautioned, "Offering price concessions can easily backfire. I'm someone who believes you should set your price fairly and only change it if you find out it is unreasonable. I've seen too many people offer to lower their price and still lose the business. There are other ways to get past the price issue."

Walt perked up at that. Several of his clients had suggested that lowering prices on products would be the best way for them to buy.

Helen saw his interest and suggested, "We've already been talking about expanding your product line. Perhaps you can offer some new products at a price point customers feel they can still afford."

"I don't see how I can provide the same level of service, or the same quality product, at a lower price," Walt countered.

"Fortunately, at a lower price point, people do not expect the same quality product or service. They are willing to trade them off for a price they consider more reasonable."

"Are you sure?" Walt questioned

Helen smiled, understanding this is a new concept to those who have heard for years that quality is the most important aspect of continued sales. "Have you heard of the *Tiffany Effect*? Even during times of economic crisis, many still want to buy jewelry. They can go to a high end jewelry store, such as Tiffany's, which offers very expensive jewelry, as well as lower priced items. Customers on a budget will look at the expensive jewelry but buy the lower priced items. If they are embarrassed to buy inexpensive jewelry at an expensive store, they may go to a department store to shop. The ones caught in the middle are high end jewelry stores which don't carry any inexpensive items. When customers have less disposable income, these stores may see sales drop off dramatically. You need to make sure your customers know you have products at a variety of prices."

After a pause to contemplate the concept, Walt started. "Let me get this straight. Since my customers are going through some tough times, they probably won't spend as much, but they still want to buy?"

"That's right. What can you do to produce the *Tiffany Effect*? What can you offer that will meet immediate customers' needs less expensively? For instance, can you offer them ways to update what they bought before?"

Walt was having trouble understanding the concept. "Can you give me an example?"

"Think of the products you've sold. Is there an upgrade to those products which can make them more useful to clients? Even high quality knives need sharpening occasionally. There is probably something you can offer which will *sharpen* your products."

"Hmmm. That makes sense."

Helen continued, "Years ago, my father used to have a business selling machines that labeled envelopes. When times were good, lots of orders for machines came in. But when times got tough, he had to sell something different: preventative maintenance. Addressing machines were finicky and customers could not afford to go without them for long. Inevitably, customers in different cities would need work on the same day, so someone had to go without. On those days, my dad could easily sell maintenance contracts, since customers with contracts went to the top of the list."

"Good story, Helen, but some of my clients claim they can't buy today because they don't have cash on hand to pay. Unless they free up some money, they are too strapped. Any suggestions for that?"

"That's the next part of my father's story," Helen frowned.

"Oops, sorry. Please continue." Walt was slightly embarrassed.

"Customers have to carefully balance their cash-flow during tough times. My father actually offered more terms in lean times than in good ones. Customers got the service they needed with less cash up front."

Walt thought that over for a minute, but his face was holding a frown. "I'm afraid my clients are going to be out of business before they can pay me."

Helen agreed, "That's a real possibility. My father would service, but not sell, equipment on credit. That way, if the clients went under, he lost some of his time and gas money, but nothing else out of his wallet."

"But others have warned me not to take credit," he debated.

"As long as people are willing to pay your prices up front, great. But if they're not..." Helen paused in mid-sentence for effect. "It is not for everyone, that's for sure. But you may be missing an opportunity."

"I know I must be missing lots of opportunities," Walt retorted. "I'm sure there are some right in front of me that I'm ignoring."

"I'll point out one," Helen remarked. "Take a look around, Walt. Do you see how many people are here in Yellow Wood? That is a sign that there is still money being spent. But remember when the owner mentioned that her revenue dropped quite a bit since the recession hit this area. There are still almost as many customers but many have cut back the amount they are spending, such as ordering drip coffee instead of cappuccinos."

He knew his mentor was trying to make an important point, but didn't get it.

"People are willing to spend a little if it will help them feel good. Even those on tight budgets keep coming to Yellow Wood rather than staying home. Couples are still buying birthday presents and going out to eat because they are willing to spend some money on things that make them feel better, and forget about the economy for a while."

When Walt still looked a bit confused, she asked point blank, "Can you offer any inexpensive products that will help people feel like they are still successful and they are still in the game?"

"Um....I never thought about something like that," Walt was taken aback that he should offer "feel-good" items in addition to his very practical portfolio.

Helen explained, "You know your customers. You know what they need. Can you offer something that may not be as practical but could still make them happy? There is a charming side of people which is much more emotional, and impractical. It really helps

them get through tough periods. So you may
want to consider it."

Glancing at her watch, "I've got another
meeting in a half hour, so I've got to run. But I
put this little list of 8 suggestions together last
night. Consider this your homework, to be
started before we meet again. Same time next
week?"

Walt nodded in assent as he took the list. He
was trying to read it while he still had a
chance to ask questions, but when he looked
up she was already striding purposefully out
the door.

8 Suggestions for Offering New Products to Existing Customers

1. Identify the products and services that you KNOW your customers still need, even when hunkered down.

2. Talk to your customers and ask open-ended questions to understand what they need today.

3. Identify additional products that they will buy, even in trying times.

4. Look at add-ons to what they already have, such as maintenance agreements or training.

5. Take advantage of the Tiffany Effect by offering items in a wide range of prices.

6. Consider offering terms, such as lease or payment terms. Remember to keep the risk down and don't offer more than you can afford to absorb.

7. Put some "feel good" products into your line.

8. Be very cautious about lowering prices excessively.

As Walt waited for Helen at Yellow Wood for their next meeting, he looked at the various antiques on the walls and thought of the skills it took to make them.

During times of economic upheaval, did those craftspeople suffer, or did they find a way to get past it until things stabilized again? Where did they get advice? Did they only have stories passed down generation to generation, or did they have mentors, like Helen, who showed them an easier way?

By the time Helen joined him, he had developed both an admiration for previous generations of professionals and a jealousy of working in a less complicated time.

Once she had settled and received her tea, he started, "I called a few customers. Unfortunately, they still don't need my products and what they do need I can't offer with any confidence."

"It is great that you made the calls, Walt. I know it is not the best news, but it is still information you can use. Do you think it is valid for all of your customers, or just a small subset?"

"I'm afraid most of my customers would be in the same boat - or should I say in the same raft floating down a river..."

"Either phrase probably would fit," Helen speculated. "So, what are you planning to do?"

"I'm hoping you have a secret that will give me some options."

Helen assured him, "My old mentor did have a few words of wisdom. Are you ready to hear them?"

Walt opened his notepad and put his pen at the ready, "All set!"

Survival Secret 5:
Find New Customers

"If your existing customers aren't in a position to buy any more, you'll have to get new customers," Helen began.

Walt interrupted, "I thought you said I shouldn't be looking for new customers?"

Helen corrected him, "I said you should try to sell to your existing customers first. Getting new customers is expensive. Even so, you'll constantly need some new customers to make up for the attrition of existing ones."

"I guess that is what you said," Walt conceded. "Where can I find new clients?"

Helen held up her hand. "Before we do that, let's take a look at exactly what they would be buying. You need to clearly define what it is you are selling."

"I think what I offer is pretty clear," Walt was confused.

"To whom? To potential customers who don't know you?"

Walt thought about that a moment, "Okay, let me try. I sell *peace of mind*. Once clients deal with me, they know they are working with the best. And I offer a money-back guarantee to prove it."

"But, Walt, that could be used by any company to sell just about everything: Tires, brakes, a bicycle, plumbing, or architecture."

"But isn't peace of mind important?" he challenged.

"At some point it will be important, but not yet. Right now prospective customers are more interested in knowing exactly what you are selling. Food? Furniture? Cars?"

"You know I have quite a number of things. How much can I narrow it down and still show my range?"

"Define your top one or two products, the ones you want to be known for. Different people are looking for different things," Helen emphasized. "Customers have their own reasons for purchasing a particular car. Some want status and will buy the fanciest model to make a statement. Others want reliability so they don't have to worry about maintenance issues."

Walt nodded and added, "I had a cousin who just bought a car for her family. She was interested in getting a car with the best safety record. Then, come to think of it, I had a neighbor who was very concerned gas prices would go up. He wanted a car that got great gas mileage. But don't most of us want cars that have all those features: reliability, safety, high gas mileage but still looks great?"

"Sure, they do. But generally one thing will stand out in a buyer's mind. If all the benefits are listed, they will just become confused. For instance, if you were trying to sell a high-performance car and mentioned it also gets excellent gas-mileage, you would confuse them since many drivers do not associate high-performance with fuel efficiency."

"I think I get it. If I claim too many benefits, people will think I am just bragging and probably won't be able to deliver."

"I couldn't have put it better myself," Helen agreed. "Now it's time for the acid test. Would potential clients really be willing to spend money on the benefits you are claiming in this economy? Be brutal. Picture yourself in your client's shoes without much time or money. Would you be willing to purchase based on what you've said your benefits are?"

"It's easy to picture myself in that condition," Walt wryly smiled. "I'm only going to spend money on things I really need, or will increase my revenue or decrease costs."

"That's probably right. If you aren't coming up with strong enough benefits, dig deeper. Break your products apart to try to find more specific reasons for people to buy. Then, determine the top 1-2 factors that would make a difference to your prospective clients. On the first pass, most sellers are too vague about the benefits they offer, so you need to dig deeper, get more specific, and find new things to brag about."

"How would I do that?"

Helen explained, "Break each of the benefits down into individual components. If you think increasing revenue or decreasing costs is important, then you'd better find a way to make that one of your benefits. For instance, if you had a lawn maintenance service, what benefit could convince potential clients going through economic difficulties to hire you?"

Walt thought about it for a bit, then said, "I will help you keep your lawn looking good for a reasonable price."

"I'm not sure that would convince me. But if you told me that letting my lawn turn into a field of dry hay would eventually cost me thousands of dollars, that would certainly get my attention."

"That would get mine, too," Walt agreed.

"In addition to pointing out the benefits, you need to let people know you have a *secret sauce* that will solve their issues better than anyone else."

Walt looked surprised. "Secret sauce?"

As he thought about it, he nodded. "You're right. I have a secret sauce that sets me apart from others. I like it!"

"Once you have that list of benefits and the secret sauce that sets you apart, you need to make a new, detailed list of people who may buy them. Who *NEEDS* those benefits enough to give you money?" Helen asked. "By name would be best. Otherwise, what are the characteristics they share?"

"Why so exact?"

"Many generalize the kinds of customers who can use their products, so they end up with a huge list. Narrow it down to just a few potentials who can validate the assumptions you made about the benefits. If you are correct, you should get fairly positive responses when you contact them."

"And if the response is not too positive?" Walt asked rhetorically.

"You'll get a cold shoulder," was Helen's reply. "Of course, the sale could be easier to prospective clients who are not hunkered down. They would be more open to listening to your benefits."

Walt stopped writing at that. "I thought everyone was hunkered down these days. Am I wrong?"

Helen nodded, "Yes, you are wrong this time. There are lots of people who don't feel desperate. Since many of your customers are in the same industry, and that industry is in trouble, you probably should be looking for clients in industries that are still doing well."

"Still doing well?" Walt agreed. "There are industries doing well?"

"Sure. Let's continue your example of the automobile industry," Helen suggested. "When lots of cars are being sold due to high salaries and disposable income, auto part stores and repair shops have lower sales volume. Many would rather buy new cars than fix the old. But when auto sales slump and owners keep their cars longer, auto parts and repair shops do quite well."

"So you are suggesting that when times are good for automobile dealers, frequently auto parts stores and repair shops suffer, and vice versa."

Then it hit him: "If I can find some different types of customers, ones who are still doing well in this economy, I would have customers who can still buy my products."

"Keep your eyes open for those clients from now on," Helen mentored. "Look around. Most people are still spending money. Instead of eating a casserole at home, they will go to a moderately priced restaurant on occasion. They may not be spending extravagantly, but they are spending."

"I have noticed that most of the restaurant parking lots seem full on Friday and Saturday nights," Walt acknowledged.

"There are groups not affected the same way by this economy. Identify them and consider how your product would interest them. Don't assume they are driven by the same needs as other clients. Make a concerted effort to find the fit between their needs and the benefits you can offer."

"But how do I find those groups?" Walt queried.

"You need to ask."

"Ask who?"

"Ask everybody. Many people ignore that huge resource at their disposal."

Walt sat up, with a slightly confused look on his face. "What do you mean?"

Helen continued. "I mean, we all know to ask current customers for referrals and leads, right? But what about vendors?" Helen asked. "Who is closer to what's going on in your industry than someone trying to sell to it? Have you talked with your vendors about what they're noticing? What do they know about current buying patterns?"

"Hmm, I hadn't considered suppliers, but it makes sense," Walt agreed.

"And don't stop there," Helen said. "Talk to others when you are networking. And, the next time you talk with your friends, ask them how they'd describe a good customer for you."

"Well, I usually don't bring up 'shop talk' with my friends."

"Your friends want you to succeed," Helen pointed out. "And they know others who know potential clients. It's the 'six degrees of separation' idea, except that in the business world the next new customer is usually closer than that. It could be as close as one degree of separation. That is, the person you ask could very well work next to someone who needs your products."

Walt finished writing, "ask everyone" on his paper, sat back and took a sip of his now cold coffee. "Anything else?"

Helen nodded. "Looking for new customers is a perfect opportunity for you to find new ways to do things. This is your business, your life. You need to be constantly looking for new ways to solve the issues that will be coming up."

"Oh, you mean *Think outside of the box?*" Walt asked.

"That's right. All entrepreneurs need to go beyond what is familiar. Even during our conversation, you've probably eliminated several groups in your head based on previous assumptions. You've got to continually challenge those assumptions to make sure you are not eliminating potentially great customers."

Helen checked her watch. "This has been a great conversation. It even reminded me of some things I need to start doing again. Shall we meet at the same time next week?"

Walt nodded, a bit lost in thought of how he could think outside the box he'd made.

Helen got half-way to the door before she remembered something. She came back, fumbling through her bag. "I almost forgot to give you these 8 hints. Here they are."

With that, she was gone.

8 Hints for Finding New Customers

1. Look for customers who need to buy your products now.

2. Redefine your products for people who don't know them.

3. Clearly specify the benefits customers will get after they buy your product.

4. Ensure the benefits are strong enough for people to open their pocket books in this economy. If not, dig deeper for more important benefits.

5. Describe the Secret Sauce you use.

6. Find groups not adversely affected by this economy and use benefits that would appeal directly to them.

7. Ask, ask, ask.

8. Think outside the box, beyond the comfortable and familiar.

The following week, Helen had already ordered before Walt arrived. As he got settled, she remarked, "When I get a chance, I like to just sit here and take a breath."

"I know what you mean. Sometimes I find it very difficult to take even a few minutes to relax," Walt disclosed. "Any time I can just sit back is something special these days." They ruminated about the burden of running their own businesses while waiting for Walt's coffee.

Then Walt showed her the new descriptions and benefits of his products. He had used them to identify prospective clients who would still use his products in this economy.

"Walt, these look great! You did a lot of good work here," Helen said with sincerity and encouragement in her voice.

"But I'm still having a problem reaching them. I know you aren't big on marketing to large groups, so I will aim just at a smaller segment. I'm thinking of having some brochures designed and printed, buying a list of names, mailing the brochures, then having a telemarketer follow up. What do you think?"

Helen hesitated before replying. "That is pretty ambitious. What kind of budget do you have?"

Walt smiled. "I knew you'd ask that question. Even though I don't have much money, as soon as this economy improves, I want to be in a position to leapfrog back into the game. As the old saying goes, *the early bird gets the worm.*"

Helen countered, "The early bird may get the first worm, but it also meets the dangers first, and could become the first casualty. There are plenty of worms out there. What happens if things don't improve for quite a while, Walt?"

"You mean up to six months?" Walt asked hopefully. "I hope it doesn't take that long."

"It could be years," Helen warned.

Survival Secret 6:
Market During Tough Times

"There's no way it could be years!" Walt protested. "I can't afford to market that long, unless sales start pouring in."

"No, you probably can't afford a broad media campaign for very long," Helen agreed.

"Then what do you suggest?" Walt asked.

"You've done a good job of identifying potential clients, but you haven't tested the accuracy of your assumptions. That is a lot like shooting in the dark - using money instead of ammunition."

"Helen, I've got a list of over 100 potential clients who need my products. Once I get in touch with them, the rest should be easy. How hard can it be to market to them?"

As the words were coming out of his mouth, Walt wished he could retract them. Sure enough, Helen immediately called him on it. "If it is so easy, why do larger companies have marketing departments and pay marketing consultants?"

Walt put his hands up in surrender. "I take it back. It may not be that easy."

"Let me see your marketing plan," Helen commanded.

Walt wrinkled his brow at the same time his mouth was forming a frown. The result was a wrinkled grimace. After a few moments his face relaxed slightly. When Helen didn't fill in the silence that had enveloped them, he shook his head slightly, took a sip of his coffee, and finally sat back in his chair.

"This may be hard to believe, Helen, but I don't have a marketing plan."

After his face had shown such anguish, the reply was so calm, that Helen couldn't help but laugh. "I'll bet most small companies don't have a marketing plan, and that is one of the reasons they suffer. Without a plan, much of your marketing efforts will probably be wasted. You can spend a lot of money without getting the results you need. How did you market in the past?"

"I knew some of my clients before I even started; they gave me referrals, and others I got through word of mouth. I don't have a lot of experience marketing, period."

"Then you have three major obstacles to overcome, in addition to the normal marketing issues," Helen explained. "First, you are trying to reach a new group of customers with which you don't have prior experience. You don't even know what their hot buttons are for sure. Second, you have very limited experience marketing, so you have a steep learning curve. In this case, that means *expensive*. And third, the economic conditions we are facing probably mean that sales cycles are much longer than normal."

Walt looked at her, "You don't make it seem too easy, Helen."

"It's not easy. But with a clear, concise marketing plan, you can focus all of your energies toward one goal. Consider using a magnifying glass to set a twig on fire. You can do it on a sunny day, but only if you have focused the light of the sun on one spot. After it catches fire, you can try to make it bigger, but you need to ignite that twig first."

"How do I ignite my twig?"

"Identify your first twig, in this case, your first potential client."

"Only one? But I've already got it narrowed down to over a hundred. Why do I have to narrow it more?" Walt demanded.

"You've got limited resources. Don't squander them trying to reach everyone on your list. Narrowing it down to one customer will make it readily apparent whether your plan will work or not. This is new to you. You will be making mistakes. Accept that. Then make inexpensive mistakes that you can afford and you'll still have resources left to reach others."

"Okay. Let's assume I will begin with ABC, Inc."

"Who will make the buying decision in that organization?"

He grimaced, and then decided to go to the top: "The CEO."

"Your next step is to find a simple, effective message. You can look at the benefits you've drawn up over the last week and decide which is most likely to get your target to request more information."

Walt was dutifully taking notes.

"Next, you can decide on how you will get your message to the prospective client. What is the best way to reach that customer?"

"As I mentioned earlier, I plan to have brochures printed and mailed, then have a telemarketer follow up with a telephone call."

"That is a form of traditional advertising. Don't forget about the Internet or networking."

Walt thought about it. "But I thought that traditional advertising was still the most effective?"

"Marketing technology is changing. Until a few years ago, the primary marketing method was traditional advertising. That includes direct mail, Yellow Pages, newspapers, magazines, radio and, the king, television. It was generally expensive, because lots of companies are competing for relatively few spots to reach their audience. The biggest budgets got the biggest bang."

"Isn't that the way it still is?"

"Yes and no. The biggest budgets may get more bang in traditional media, but the number of choices where buyers can get information has changed the playing field. Years ago there were three television stations available, now there are hundreds. There are more magazines available today than ever before. And the Internet has taken choice to a whole new level. As a result, marketing is in flux. Much of what we understood last year has changed this year. The Internet is still changing so rapidly that businesses large and small are still catching up.

"I do have a website, Helen. Maybe I should be doing Internet marketing instead."

"Having a website is important, but it is just the beginning. To do Internet marketing, you need to draw people to your site. There are lots of ways to do that, some expensive, some cheap."

"And some are free," Walt added.

"Not really. No matter what you do, you'll be spending time or money developing a campaign. There are lots of providers who will sell services to you, including web advertising, search engine optimization techniques, blogs, and much more. "

"How about social media? I've started to dabble in that."

"Social Media is a broad, encompassing category that includes content, experiential media, mobile networks, and a wide realm of services. People are constantly looking for new ways to connect. In fact, when they are looking for solutions to problems or for things to buy, they frequently ask others electronically for advice. Like I said, the marketing landscape is in flux, and will be for years."

"The Internet has gotten so complicated that I probably need to hire someone if my Internet marketing is going to be effective. I wonder if there is another way I can market my product on a shoe string."

"Actually there is. Although it is time-intensive, it is inexpensive money-wise, yet still can be the most effective way of selling yourself: Networking."

Walt grimaced. "Have I told you I'm shy, and don't like networking events?"

"Most business people don't, at least initially. Once you get used to them, you will be fine. Just remember that the key to true business networking is establishing a mutually beneficial relationship. The most important skill for effective business networking is listening; focusing on how you can help the person you are listening to rather than on how he or she can help you."

"I wonder if I could network with the CEO of ABC, Inc.?" thought Walt.

"Once you do connect, your end goal is to get those people to ask for more information about you and your products. How will they get that information? Will it be by calling you on the telephone, writing to you, going to your website, or what?" she grilled him.

"I do a LOT of my research over the Internet these days, and I assume that is how most people would do it. I have a website, as you know, but it needs some work."

"Does it paint an accurate picture of you and your products?" she pushed. "Does it have testimonials from former clients? Is your best product highlighted? The best way to make sure you are on the right track is to look at your marketing material through your clients' eyes," Helen coached. "Pretend you are a client in the buying process. What would you want to know about you and your product?"

"Okay, I can do that. I've already been looking at other people's websites to see what they've done.

"Don't forget to have others look at yours. It never hurts to have another set of eyes looking. I was talking to a marketer who specializes in branding. After her new website was up and running, someone mentioned that her brand logo was not on it. Boy, was she embarrassed."

Walt retorted, "I'll bet she was. I've made mistakes like that before and I'm sure I'll make them again."

"We all have, Walt. The secret, of course, is to keep away from costly mistakes. Fixing website mistakes is usually straightforward and simple. But correcting a mistake on 2,000 brochures can get expensive."

"I see your point, Helen."

"Going back to my earlier question, what is your budget?"

"How much do I need?" was Walt's reply.

"Unless you have almost unlimited funds, that is the wrong question. That is the way many entrepreneurs decide how much to spend. They take a stab at an effective program, then they implement it, and then they find out it costs much more than they estimated."

Walt tried to keep his face from revealing that he might have done that exact thing.

Helen ignored Walt's twitch and went on. "There's a common saying about packing for vacations, *Pack early, then take out half the clothes but carry twice as much money.* The same is true for marketing, cut your expectations in half, and expect it to cost twice as much."

"That makes it seem as if I can hardly do anything," Walt complained. "I really need to get going."

"I'd recommend you get going but start small, and then measure, measure, measure. Measure as much as you can. Measure how much it costs for each stage of the program. Measure how many people were reached and actually looked at your material. Measure the amount of business that was generated by any particular program."

Walt realized he had more work than he expected.

"Here are 8 criteria for setting up an effective marketing plan." Then she handed Walt a folded piece of paper. "Does the same time next week work?"

Walt told her, "Absolutely!"

After she left Yellow Wood, Walt unfolded the paper to see what she had written about marketing.

8 Criteria for Marketing During Tough Times

1. Design a coordinated marketing plan.

2. Narrow your target, initially to one client.

3. Settle on the simplest message that will attract attention.

4. Determine the medium - Traditional advertising, Internet, or Networking.

5. Set up a system for prospective clients to find out more about you and your products.

6. Look at everything through the eyes of your customers.

7. Use a budget - then assume you can only get half as much done and it will cost twice as much as your budget.

8. Measure, measure, measure.

After a week of setting up a marketing plan, Walt was ready for a break. He arrived at the cafe early and relaxed until Helen was ready to begin the session. Then he started, "I put together a marketing plan, but every time I think about implementing some part of it, I realize how many other things I need. I didn't realize how difficult it would be to market my business!"

Helen laughed. "You've had a week and it's not done?"

"Hmmm. Do you think I overestimated how much I could get done?" he asked facetiously.

"Now you can begin to appreciate how much time and effort can go into marketing. Then, even with huge budgets, returns are not guaranteed."

"What I didn't understand was how many things have to fit together to make a good marketing plan."

"Join the club. Marketing is one of those things that we all have to learn, usually the hard way. Of course, the more you do it, the easier it becomes," she encouraged. "All of the time you are spending is an investment so you'll be ready for the next *business cycle*."

"Business cycle?" Walt realized he was about to find out about one more Business Survival Secret.

Business Survival Secret 7: Prepare For The Next Business Cycle

"I'm sure you know, Walt, that everything goes through cycles," Helen began. "In fact, understanding cycle theory is a major secret to maintaining a successful business over the long term. Economic cycles are great while going up, but everything that goes up must come down."

Walt nodded. "I started my business on an up-cycle a few years ago, and success seemed so easy. You know how they say *a rising tide lifts all ships*. I was riding the tide!"

"Next time it will probably help to remember that the opposite is also true: *A falling tide drops all ships*." Helen warned, "The higher and longer the up cycle is, the lower and longer the down-cycle will be."

Letting out a deep breath, he sounded like a deflating balloon.

Helen nodded compassionately, and went on. "There are economic cycles and industrial cycles. And every company goes through its own cycles. For instance, the United States seems to go through an economic cycle every eight to ten years, beginning with a major upsurge which is followed by a recession."

"Well, the upsurge over the last few years was good for me," Walt noted. "I thought everything was going great. Even when I saw the national economy start to soften, our local economy still seemed to be doing great."

"Depending on where you live and what industries are located nearby, the local economy may lead the cycle, or can follow it. A lot of times, state and local governments are a year or two behind the economic cycle because they only budget what they get in taxes, but don't get to collect it for a year after the budget is implemented. If there is a lot of government spending in your area, it can prop up the local economy for a while. Then again, after much of the rest of the economy has recovered from a recession or such, it could be a year or so behind before they catch up."

"That makes sense," Walt agreed.

"Another very important factor to watch is the industry you are in. For instance, high technology tends to go in cycles of 15 years or so. For a few years, high tech seems to stagnate. Then something will happen and it begins to grow stratospherically. New ages of prosperity are predicted. In actuality, the industry can't keep up with the hype, and investors who expect continued strong growth are suddenly in trouble as reality hits."

Walt noted he had fallen into that trap before.

Helen kept on, "Just as importantly, companies operate in cycles, too. There are a lot of things that go on during the life cycle of a company, but I'll keep it simple and highlight the Startup, Growth, Mature, and Renewal or Decline phases.

Walt opened to a fresh sheet of paper and started writing, while Helen explained, "In the Startup phase, you're getting your company going, but have limited revenue. During the Growth phase of the business life cycle, orders accelerate as more customers want to buy the products. In many cases, workers are spending most of their time and resources just filling orders and it pushes the infrastructure of the company to its limit."

"I guess my company was in the 'Growth' part of my life cycle," Walt observed. "It was kind of crazy, but it sure felt good."

"Maybe, but businesses that are not solidly built can suffer terribly when orders slow down."

Walt sighed. "I knew my orders were going to slow down some day, but I still wasn't prepared."

Helen nodded in sympathy, then continued, "When a company makes it to the Mature phase, it actually has a strong foundation and can take some hits without too much trauma. However, after a while, it has to Renew itself or it will Decline, and may self-destruct."

"I haven't made it to the Mature stage yet, but I still need to "Renew" my business," Walt pointed out.

"Look for indicators of where your market is going, up or down. Read trade magazines and talk to people in the know. If you can get an early indication of where your market is going, you can be prepared. For instance, an indicator of the national economy could be the financial services industry, of which the stock market is part. When investors feel confident, they will start investing more, including in the stock market. Additional investments give larger companies confidence to spend more, which in turn helps other companies get more revenue and also spend more."

"Well, I did pay attention to the financial news, trying to predict how long the good times would go on."

"The news is only one source, and not even a particularly good one. Headlines are intended to play on emotions, to get readers hooked. They tend to be either euphoric or doom and gloom. You need to be constantly reading and listening to knowledgeable people if you are going to predict what is going to happen."

"Okay, Helen. Let me get this straight. Each business, including mine, has a number of cycles that affect it, including the world economy, the local economy, the industry, and even its own internal ups and downs."

"That's right," Helen answered.

"How can a business survive if the world is so unpredictable?" wondered Walt aloud.

Helen smiled. "It's really not as hard as it seems. Fortunately, when businesses prepare for any one cycle, they are actually setting up a survival plan that covers many cycles. If you continually try to predict how the business environment will change over the next three months to a year, you will notice the changes that many miss. Then, you will have contingency plans in place before orders dry up."

He thought about that for a few moments, then added, "And while I've got time, I should be thinking about what customers will need as they begin the next cycle."

"Right on, Walt."

"I think I understand your cycle theory, Helen. But I don't see how it helps me now. My business is barely hanging on."

"If nothing else, you can keep an eye on companies that are on opposite cycles. We talked about them a couple weeks ago. If you can identify some of those companies, you can have clients that are on different cycles."

"Hmmmm," Walt pondered. "If I had known all this before, I would have seen this economic slowdown coming. Then I could have looked for customers who were going to do well in the changing marketplace."

"That is correct. Even if you could not find the right client mix, you would not make purchases on credit unless they were absolutely necessary. And you would be in a much stronger position now."

"So, if I understand this, when things were going particularly well, I should have started preparing for the worst?" Walt asked.

"Absolutely correct. As Intel's Andy Grove said, *Only the paranoid survive.* Warren Buffet uses a general rule, *'Be fearful when others are greedy, and be greedy when others are fearful.'* In other words, if everyone says that times are good, prepare for the worst. If everyone says that times are terrible, prepare to ride the wave of prosperity."

"Wait a second, Helen. I think you are telling me two things - to prepare for boom times, but at the same time - be very cautious."

"That's right. With the proper mindset and planning, you'll be able to weather the future storms and be ready to sell like crazy when the environment is right."

As Walt thought about that, she reached into her bag and pulled out a sheet of paper, replying "Look at these 8 pointers and see if they make sense."

8 Steps to Prepare for the Next Business Cycle

1. Determine where the national economy is going: Up, down or steady.

2. See how the local economy is being affected.

3. Find out if your particular industry is growing, stable, or retracting.

4. Decide if you are in the Startup, Growth, Mature, Renewal or Decline phase.

5. Look for indicators of where things are going. Never use only one source, and try to not pay attention to the headlines.

6. Based on the above information, make an action plan for the next 3, 6 & 12 months.

7. Identify clients who are in opposite cycles so you can always have strong prospects in your pipeline.

8. Be a little paranoid. Always keep some resources in reserve.

Walt spent the next few days trying to identify the various cycles that affected his business. He looked at the national and local economies, as well as the industries his clients were in. While it was not all bad news, it was obvious that it could be months before he could expect lucrative contracts from his former clients.

At their next meeting, he explained this all to Helen. She was impressed at how calm his composure remained, "You're able to take bad news much better now than when we first met, a couple months ago."

Walt thought about that before replying, "Both mentally and emotionally, I am in a much better place than before. I was especially stressed because I had no way to deal with the changes. I felt like I had no options. At least now I've got a long list of things to do."

Then his demeanor changed. "The question is whether I have the right stuff to make it through more storms in the future. I'm wondering if I should start looking for a *real job*, as some of my friends and relatives are suggesting. I'm meeting more and more business owners who just could not make it. I might never be successful."

"It sounds as if you are at a fork in the road, Walt. This is as good a time as any to make the decision of whether to keep being your own boss, with all the pitfalls and dangers associated with that, or whether it is time to become an employee again. If you are going to get out, do it while you still have some resources."

"The problem is, Helen, I really don't want to get out. Do you think I have what it takes to make it?"

Survival Secret 8:
Never Give Up

Helen cocked her head, "Your ability to succeed as a small business owner depends on how much you are willing to fight. Lots of people want to have their own business, but only a few are willing to sacrifice and struggle enough to become successful."

"I am willing to fight, Helen. Now that I've had my own business and have been my own boss, I can't imagine going back as an employee again. Just the thought of it makes me depressed. I really want to make it!"

"Good. The great football coach, Vince Lombardi, once told his players, *Winning isn't everything, but wanting to win is.* It's going to be an uphill battle, but persistence can overcome a lot of other shortcomings."

Walt said, "Of course, I assume there is some chance that I will actually reach my dream goals."

"You can, if you work hard enough. Determination is important, since three-fourths of all the companies started this year will not be around in five years.

"That's some pep talk you're giving me, Helen."

"The news is not actually as bad as all that. Some companies merge and others were just short term ventures. Still, a lot fail, probably 50% or more.

"So there is still only a 50:50 chance I will be successful?" Walt realized.

"With any one venture, yes. But the total number of successful ventures is increasing by a million or more each year in the US. What that really means is: After their first setback, a lot of those founders learned their lessons, licked their wounds, then rolled up their sleeves and started another venture."

"Really? That many found a way to make it after a failure?"

"That's right, Walt. All the successful entrepreneurs I've known have learned their business skills the hard way. Many of them started 2 or 3 companies before finding the right combination of factors to become successful. I've never met an entrepreneur who was a natural success. In fact, their initial failure was probably a major reason for their eventual success."

Walt thought a moment. "That's a much better story. I'm looking for reassurances that I can make it."

"It's not easy," Helen warned. "It takes a lot of fortitude to keep getting up in the morning, realizing it will be another day of learning hard lessons."

"Well, I'm in the learning mode. But I wonder if it is worth trying to grow under these economic conditions."

Helen hesitated. "It seems pretty tough, doesn't it? Yet a wealthy entrepreneur once told me that more millionaires were created during the Great Depression than any other period in our nation's history."

Walt's eyes widened. "During the Great Depression? How did they do it?"

"Many of them had money saved up, so they could buy businesses for pennies on the dollar. But others had no money and still became household names. One grandfather started selling fried chicken at his gas station, calling it Kentucky Fried Chicken. In 1939, Bill Hewlett and Dave Packard started their business with only $538. And there are thousands of others who saw opportunities while others were despairing."

"Wow. I thought most of the stories were like Steinbeck's *Grapes of Wrath*," Walt exclaimed.

"No," Helen shook her head. "While there were millions of people seriously affected by the Great Depression, many still kept their eyes open for opportunities. Speaking of opportunities, did you know that the word *Crisis* in Chinese is actually two symbols together? One is *danger*, the other is *opportunity*."

"My company is still in crisis, and I hope there are real opportunities. I know I am still in danger of losing lots of money."

Helen sympathized, "I'd recommend you always have three exit plans, one for regular growth of your business, a second in case it takes off like a rocket, and a third in case it begins to sink and needs to be abandoned. If you don't see this venture making a good profit, shutting it down is a solid business decision."

"Man, I hate to do that. I've already invested so much time and money."

"Well you've learned a lot of lessons. Remember, long-term success comes to those who keep trying."

"*Keep on trying.* That sounds like something my mother used to tell me. And she also said, *When the going gets tough, the tough get going.*"

Helen nodded her head, in agreement. "Disraeli said *There is no education like adversity.* Small business owners do well by remembering it's the journey, not the destination. Then, you can look behind you and see how far you actually have come. That helps you get psyched up for the next part of your journey."

"That's true," agreed Walt. "Looking back at how much I've learned over the last few months makes me feel a bit more confident. I've still got a lot to learn, but these changes should help make my company strong again."

Helen waited a moment before changing the topic, "I've got something else to tell you: This is our last meeting for a while. For almost a year I have been developing relationships with some influential businesses, and I just closed contracts with two of them. They will be taking all of my time for the next few months, including a lot of travel."

"What? You're leaving me?" was Walt's initial reaction.

"I think you are well on your way to major successes, Walt. I know you'll press on."

Then Helen rustled around in her bag, brought out a notebook. She searched through it, looking for something between the pages. Finally, she found a folded sheet of paper and handed it to him.

Walt carefully unfolded the fragile paper that she had obviously been carrying for years, and found some words of wisdom. "Wow!" was all he had to say after reading it. "Can I write them down?"

"No. You can have it! I have had it quite a while and I've got a copy. I got it from my mentor. After you have become successful, you can give it to someone else who needs it."

Then, with a quick hug, she was gone. Walt sat back down and looked over the list...

8 Survival Quotations

1. Winning isn't everything, but wanting to win is. -- Vince Lombardi

2. Happy are those who dream dreams and are ready to pay the price to make them come true. -- Leon J. Suenes

3. Every artist was first an amateur. -- Ralph Waldo Emerson

4. Misfortunes often sharpen the genius. -- Ovid

5. Our greatest glory is not in never falling but in rising every time we fall. -- Confucius

6. There is no education like adversity. -- Benjamin Disraeli

7. Fractures well cured make us more strong. -- Ralph Waldo Emerson

8. Nothing in this world can take the place of persistence. Talent will not; nothing is more common than unsuccessful people with talent. Genius will not; unrewarded genius is almost a proverb. Education will not; the world is full of educated derelicts. Persistence and determination alone are omnipotent. The slogan 'press on' has solved and always will solve the problems of the human race. -- Calvin Coolidge

Epilogue

Yellow Wood was almost the same, a year after they started meeting there. Walt was enjoying a good cappuccino, looking at the antiques on the wall. He now had a different appreciation for the hard work each entrepreneur put in to make the wares.

Helen arrived a few minutes later. "I've been working on those contracts for nine months and finally got a break. I am so glad you called. How are you doing?"

"It has been a difficult journey, Helen, but I'm still in business. I had to completely refocus my company, but orders continue to trickle in. My bank book doesn't really show it yet, but I know I've got a much stronger business now."

As he reached down to a bag near his feet, he told her, "And this is one of the things that kept me on track."

He took out what appeared to be a photo album and handed it to her. Inside were all eight of the lists she had given him...

8 Tips to Minimize Expenditures

1. Record all expenses, personal and financial.

2. Ruthlessly eliminate everything not absolutely necessary.

3. List all recurring bills and debts to understand how much money you will need, and when.

4. Keep a journal of all ordinary expenses for several weeks, preferably a month, to show your "hidden expenses."

5. Contact all customers who owe you money and remind them that payments are due.

6. Call lenders to get best rates available.

7. Shop around and renegotiate with service providers to get the best rates possible.

8. Keep your loved ones involved.

8 Ways to Hang Onto Customers

1. Create a "customer relationship management" system to keep in regular contact with customers.

2. Develop a script, then pick up the phone and call.

3. Get personal - make it about them. You can use the FORD method: Family, Occupation, Recreation, Dreams.

4. Remember that things may have changed, so find out what their needs are today. Then you can show how your product will help meet some of those needs.

5. Identify new ways to help your clients. Ask questions like: "What would you like us to do differently?"

6. Find out how your product has been working for them.

7. Offer a Referral Reward Program.

8. Set up a repeat buyer program, such as a reduced price for two or more things purchased at the same time, or Reward Cards for points and discounts.

8 Steps to Revise Your Business Model

1. Accurately assess your current business. What are you selling? Who is buying? Does it still make sense in today's conditions?

2. Determine what has been working. (This step is very important).

3. Look at what is not working, and see if minor changes fix these issues.

4. Forecast how many of your customers will continue to buy your products in the foreseeable future.

5. Identify other high-potential customers who may need your products.

6. Talk to your customers. Confirm your assumptions.

7. Keep your eyes open for new opportunities.

8. Make a decision of how your business should operate moving forward.

8 Suggestions for Offering New Products to Existing Customers

1. 1. Identify the products and services that you KNOW your customers still need, even when hunkered down.

2. Talk to your customers and ask open-ended questions to understand what they need today.

3. Identify additional products that they will buy, even in trying times.

4. Look at add-ons to what they already have, such as maintenance agreements or training.

5. Take advantage of the Tiffany Effect by offering items in a wide range of prices.

6. Consider offering terms, such as lease or payment terms. Remember to keep the risk down and don't offer more than you can afford to absorb.

7. Put some "feel good" products into your line.

8. Be very cautious about lowering prices excessively.

8 Hints for Finding New Customers

1. Look for customers who need to buy your products now.

2. Redefine your products for people who don't know them.

3. Clearly specify the benefits customers will get after they buy your product.

4. Ensure the benefits are strong enough for people to open their pocket books in this economy. If not, dig deeper for more important benefits.

5. Describe the Secret Sauce you use.

6. Find groups not adversely affected by this economy and use benefits that would appeal directly to them.

7. Ask, ask, ask.

8. Think outside the box, beyond the comfortable and familiar.

8 Criteria for Marketing During Tough Times

1. Design a coordinated marketing plan.

2. Narrow your target, initially to one client.

3. Settle on the simplest message that will attract attention.

4. Determine the medium - Traditional advertising, Internet, or Networking.

5. Set up a system for prospective clients to find out more about you and your products.

6. Look at everything through the eyes of your customers.

7. Use a budget - then assume you can only get half as much done and it will cost twice as much as your budget.

8. Measure, measure, measure.

8 Steps to Prepare for the Next Business Cycle

1. Determine where the national economy is going: Up, down or steady.

2. See how the local economy is being affected.

3. Find out if your particular industry is growing, stable, or retracting.

4. Decide if you are in the Startup, Growth, Mature, Renewal or Decline phase.

5. Look for indicators of where things are going. Never use only one source, and try to not pay attention to the headlines.

6. Based on the above information, make an action plan for the next 3, 6 & 12 months.

7. Identify clients who are in opposite cycles so you can always have strong prospects in your pipeline.

8. Be a little paranoid. Always keep some resources in reserve.

8 Survival Quotations

1. Winning isn't everything, but wanting to win is. -- Vince Lombardi

2. Happy are those who dream dreams and are ready to pay the price to make them come true. -- Leon J. Suenes

3. Every artist was first an amateur. -- Ralph Waldo Emerson

4. Misfortunes often sharpen the genius. -- Ovid

5. Our greatest glory is not in never falling but in rising every time we fall. -- Confucius

6. There is no education like adversity. -- Benjamin Disraeli

7. Fractures well cured make us more strong. -- Ralph Waldo Emerson

8. Nothing in this world can take the place of persistence. Talent will not; nothing is more common than unsuccessful people with talent. Genius will not; unrewarded genius is almost a proverb. Education will not; the world is full of educated derelicts. Persistence and determination alone are omnipotent. The slogan 'press on' has solved and always will solve the problems of the human race. -- Calvin Coolidge

Acknowledgments

I would like to thank those colleagues who shared their experiences and offered their expertise, especially members of the ExecNet group of small business CEOs.

Many friends helped with this book, including Nina Smith, Marge Jensen, Tom Leal and Lisa Nichols.

I especially want to thank my wife, Sandy, for all the love she provided through the months that I was holed up working on this book. She also became the primary editor, reading and suggesting changes to the manuscript untold times. Without her support, it probably never would have been finished.

About the Author

Steven Hilferty is a Small Business Success Coach. Before entering the world of business, Steven was a U.S. Coast Guard rescue helicopter pilot and saved over 200 lives. He managed teams of over 150 people at various air stations, and directed the operations of over 2,000 Coast Guard Auxiliarists.

Steven earned his MBA at Georgetown University, followed by several years of consulting with clients ranging from startups to Fortune 500 companies. He became an executive coach specializing in small businesses in 2000. When not working with small business owners, he teaches the capstone course for MBA students, *Strategies For Competitive Advantage*.

For more information
and inquiries about quantity discounts,
please contact:

Business Coach Press
48 Mathews Place
Alamo, CA 94507
USA

800-507-2450
925-262-8936

info@8survivalsecrets.com

www.8SurvivalSecrets.com

.

www.ingramcontent.com/pod-product-compliance
Lightning Source LLC
Chambersburg PA
CBHW020208200326
41521CB00005BA/290